THIS WALKER BOOK BELONGS TO:

_____

_____

_____

_____

Acknowledgements
With the exception of Lewis Carroll, Hilaire
Belloc, Samuel Goodrich and Edward Lear, the authors
of the rhymes in this book are unknown.
Thanks are due for permission to reprint the following
copyright material: "The Elephant", "The Frog" and "The Lion"
by Hilaire Belloc (published in *Selected Cautionary Verses*,
Puffin 1987) reprinted by permission of the Peters Fraser
and Dunlop Group Ltd.

First published 1990 by
Walker Books Ltd
87 Vauxhall Walk
London SE11 5HJ

Illustrations © 1990 Emma Chichester Clark

This edition published 1993

Printed in Hong Kong by
South China Printing Co. (1988) Ltd.

British Library Cataloguing in Publication Data
A catalogue record for this book is
available from the British Library.
ISBN 0-7445-3077-6

I never saw a purple cow

and other nonsense rhymes

Emma Chichester Clark

WALKER BOOKS
LONDON

For William

A CAT CAME FIDDLING

A cat came fiddling out of a barn,
With a pair of bag-pipes under her arm;
She could sing nothing but Fiddle cum fee,
The mouse has married the bumble-bee.
Pipe, cat; dance, mouse;
We'll have a wedding at our good house.

THE OWL AND THE PUSSY-CAT

The Owl and the Pussy-cat went to sea
   In a beautiful pea-green boat;
They took some honey, and plenty of money,
   Wrapped up in a five-pound note.
The Owl looked up to the stars above,
   And sang to a small guitar,
"O lovely Pussy! O Pussy, my love,
   What a beautiful Pussy you are,
      You are,
      You are!
What a beautiful Pussy you are!"

Pussy said to the Owl, "You elegant fowl!
　　How charmingly sweet you sing!
O let us be married! too long we have tarried:
　　But what shall we do for a ring?"
They sailed away, for a year and a day,
　　To the land where the Bong-tree grows,
And there in a wood a Piggy-wig stood,
　　With a ring at the end of his nose,
　　　His nose,
　　　His nose,
　　With a ring at the end of his nose.

"Dear Pig, are you willing to sell for one shilling
　　Your ring?" Said the Piggy, "I will."
So they took it away, and were married next day
　　By the Turkey who lives on the hill.
They dined on mince, and slices of quince,
　　Which they ate with a runcible spoon;
And hand in hand, on the edge of the sand,
　　They danced by the light of the moon,
　　　The moon,
　　　The moon,
　　They danced by the light of the moon.

Edward Lear

SING, SING

Sing, sing,
    What shall I sing?
The cat's run away
    With the pudding string!
Do, do,
    What shall I do?
The cat's run away
    With the pudding too!

THE CAT SAT ASLEEP

The cat sat asleep by the side of the fire,
    The mistress snored loud as a pig;
Jack took up his fiddle by Jenny's desire,
    And struck up a bit of a jig.

THERE WAS AN OLD PERSON OF BRAY

There was an Old Person of Bray,
Who sang through the whole of the Day
　　To his Ducks and his Pigs,
　　Whom he fed upon Figs,
That valuable Person of Bray.

Edward Lear

THERE WAS A YOUNG LADY OF BUTE

There was a Young Lady of Bute,
Who played on a silver-gilt flute;
She played several jigs
To her uncle's white pigs,
　　That amusing Young Lady of Bute.

Edward Lear

THERE WAS AN OLD MAN ON THE BORDER

There was an Old Man on the Border,
Who lived in the utmost disorder;
He danced with the Cat
And made Tea in his Hat,
　　Which vexed all the folks on the Border.

Edward Lear

THERE WAS A PIPER HAD A COW

There was a piper had a cow,
　　And he had naught to give her.
He pulled out his pipes and played her a tune,
　　And bade the cow consider.

The cow considered very well
　　And gave the piper a penny,
And bade him play the other tune,
　　"Corn rigs are bonny".

DICKERY, DICKERY, DARE

Dickery, dickery, dare,
The pig flew up in the air;
The man in brown
Soon brought him down,
Dickery, dickery, dare.

LITTLE JACK SPRAT

Little Jack Sprat
  Once had a pig;
It was not very little,
  Nor yet very big,
It was not very lean,
  It was not very fat –
It's a good pig to grunt,
  Said little Jack Sprat.

THE PETTITOES

The pettitoes are little feet,
  And the little feet not big;
Great feet belong to the grunting hog,
  And the pettitoes to the little pig.

AS I LOOKED OUT

As I looked out on Saturday last,
A fat little pig went hurrying past.
Over his shoulders he wore a shawl,
Although he didn't seem cold at all.
I waved at him, but he didn't see,
For he never so much as looked at me.
Once again, when the moon was high,
I saw the little pig hurrying by;
Back he came at a terrible pace,
The moonlight shone on his little pink face,
And he smiled with a face that was quite content.
But never I knew where that little pig went.

WHOSE LITTLE PIGS

Whose little pigs are these, these, these?
    Whose little pigs are these?
They are Roger the Cook's, I know by their looks;
    I found them among my peas.
Go pound them, go pound them.
    I dare not on my life,
For though I love not Roger the Cook,
    I dearly love his wife.

TEASING

Little Jack Horner
Sat in the corner,
Eating his curds and whey;
There came a big spider,
Who sat down beside her,
And the dish ran away with the spoon.

LITTLE MISS TUCKETT

Little Miss Tuckett
Sat on a bucket,
Eating some peaches and cream;
There came a grasshopper
And tried hard to stop her
But she said, "Go away, or I'll scream."

LITTLE POLL PARROT

Little Poll Parrot
Sat in his garret
Eating toast and tea;
A little brown mouse
Jumped into the house,
And stole it all away.

LITTLE TIM SPRAT

Little Tim Sprat
Had a pet rat,
In a tin cage with a wheel.
Said little Tim Sprat,
Each day to his rat:
If hungry, my dear, you must squeal.

FOUR AND TWENTY TAILORS

Four and twenty tailors
   Went to kill a snail.
The best man amongst them
   Durst not touch her tail;
She put out her horns
   Like a little Kyloe cow,
Run, tailors, run,
   Or she'll kill you all e'en now.

LET US GO TO THE WOODS

Let us go to the woods, says this pig.
What to do there? says this pig.
To seek mamma, says this pig.
What to do with her? says this pig.
To kiss her, to kiss her, says this pig.

A ROBIN AND A ROBIN'S SON

A robin and a robin's son
Once went to town to buy a bun.
They couldn't decide on plum or plain,
And so they went back home again.

THERE WAS AN OLD SOLDIER OF BISTER

There was an old soldier of Bister
Went walking one day with his sister,
    When a cow at one poke
    Tossed her into an oak
Before the old gentleman missed her.

A FUNNY OLD PERSON

A funny old person of Slough
Took all of his meals with a cow.
    He said, "It's uncanny,
    She's so like Aunt Fanny!"
But he never would indicate how.

RAT A TAT TAT

Rat a tat tat, who is that?
Only grandma's pussy cat.
What do you want?
A pint of milk.
Where's your money?
In my pocket.
Where's your pocket?
I forgot it.
O you silly pussy cat.

A LIZARD WRIGGLED

A lizard wriggled on his belly
To Leeds to see his Aunt Nelly.
She said, "What a long, long way you've come,
A-wriggling on your tired tum."

THE ELEPHANT IS A GRACEFUL BIRD

The elephant is a graceful bird;
  It flits from twig to twig.
It builds its nest in a rhubarb tree
  And whistles like a pig.

WAY DOWN SOUTH

Way down South where bananas grow,
A grasshopper stepped on an elephant's toe.
The elephant said, with tears in his eyes,
"Pick on somebody your own size."

THE ELEPHANT

When people call this beast to mind,
They marvel more and more
At such a LITTLE tail behind,
So LARGE a trunk before.

Hilaire Belloc

23

A MOUSE IN HER ROOM

A mouse in her room woke Miss Dowd.
She was frightened and screamed very loud.
Then a happy thought hit her –
To scare off the critter
She sat up in bed and meowed.

I RAISED A GREAT HULLABALOO

I raised a great hullabaloo
When I found a large mouse in my stew,
   Said the waiter, "Don't shout
   And wave it about,
Or the rest will be wanting one, too!"

THERE WAS A WEE BIT MOOSIKIE

There was a wee bit moosikie
That lived in a pantry-attay O.
But it couldna get a bit o' cheese
For cheekie-poussie-cattie O.
Said the mousie tae the cheesikie,
   O fain wad I be at ye O,
   If it werena' for the cruel paws
     O' cheekie-poussie-cattie O.

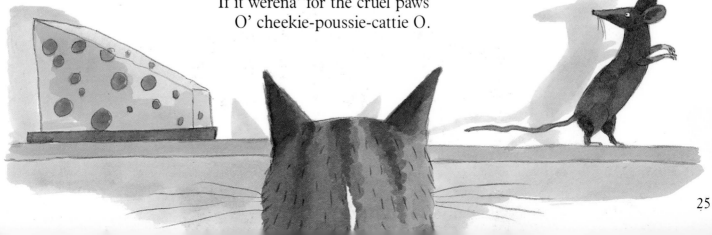

CALICO PIE

Calico Pie,
The little Birds fly
Down to the calico tree,
Their wings were blue,
And they sang "Tilly-loo!"
Till away they flew –
And they never came back to me!
They never came back!
They never came back!
They never came back to me!

Calico Jam,
The little Fish swam,
Over the syllabub sea,
He took off his hat,
To the Sole and the Sprat,
And the Willeby-wat –
But he never came back to me!
He never came back!
He never came back!
He never came back to me!

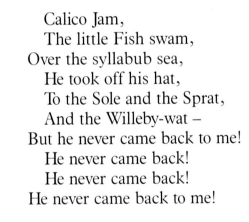

Calico Ban,
　The little Mice ran,
To be ready in time for tea,
　Flippity flup,
　They drank it all up,
　And danced in the cup –
But they never came back to me!
　They never came back!
　They never came back!
They never came back to me!

Calico Drum,
　The Grasshoppers come,
The Butterfly, Beetle and Bee,
　Over the ground,
　Around and round,
　With a hop and a bound –
But they never came back!
　They never came back!
　They never came back!
They never came back to me!

Edward Lear

A RABBIT RACED A TURTLE

A rabbit raced a turtle,
You know the turtle won;
And Mister Bunny came in late –
A little hot cross bun.

POOR DOG BRIGHT

Poor dog Bright
Ran off with all his might
Because the cat was after him
Poor dog Bright.

Poor cat Fright
Ran off with all her might
Because the dog was after her
Poor cat Fright.

RATS IN THE GARDEN

Rats in the garden, catch 'em Towser,
Cows in the cornfield, run, boys, run;
Cat's in the cream pot, stop her, now sir,
Fire on the mountain, run, boys, run.

THERE WAS A LITTLE GUINEA-PIG

There was a little guinea-pig,
Which being little was not big.
He always walked upon feet,
And never failed when he eat.

Though ne'er instructed by a cat,
He knew a mouse was not a rat;
He knew the good from naughty boys;
And when he squealed he made a noise.

When from a place he ran away,
He never at that place did stay;
And when he ran as I am told,
He never stood still for young or old.

One day I heard it gravely said,
That Master guinea-pig was dead;
If that's the case, we safely may
Conclude he's not alive today.

MARY WENT DOWN TO GRANDPA'S FARM

Mary went down to Grandpa's farm;
The billy goat chased her round the barn,
Chased her up the sycamore tree,
And this is the song she sang to me:
"I like coffee, I like tea,
I like the boys and the boys like me."

AS I WAS GOING O'ER TIPPLE TINE

As I was going o'er Tipple Tine,
I met a flock of bonny swine;
  Some yellow necked,
  Some yellow backed,
They were the very bonniest swine
That went over Tipple Tine.

AS I WENT UP THE HIGH HILL

As I went up the high hill,
There I saw a climbing goat;
I went down by the running rill,
There I saw a ragged sheep;
I went out to the roving sea,
There I saw a tossing boat;
I went under the green tree,
There I saw two doves asleep.

AS I WENT OVER THE WATER

As I went over the water,
The water went over me,
I saw two little blackbirds sitting on a tree:
The one called me a rascal,
The other one called me a thief;
I took up my little black stick,
And knocked out all their teeth.

AS I WAS WALKING ROUND THE LAKE

As I was walking round the lake
I met a little rattlesnake,
I gave him so much ice-cream cake
It made his little belly ache.

AS I WENT TO BONNER

As I went to Bonner,
   I met a pig
    Without a wig,
Upon my word and honour.

A FOX JUMPED UP

A fox jumped up one winter's night,
And begged the moon to give him light,
For he'd many miles to trot that night
Before he reached his den O!
    Den O! Den O!
For he'd many miles to trot that night
Before he reached his den O!

The first place he came to was a farmer's yard,
Where the ducks and the geese declared it hard
That their nerves should be shaken and their rest so marred
By a visit from Mr Fox O!
    Fox O! Fox O!
That their nerves should be shaken and their rest so marred
By a visit from Mr Fox O!

He took the grey goose by the neck,
And swung him right across his back;
The grey goose cried out, Quack, quack, quack,
With his legs hanging dangling down O!
    Down O! Down O!
The grey goose cried out, Quack, quack, quack,
With his legs hanging dangling down O!

Old Mother Slipper Slopper jumped out of bed,
And out of the window she popped her head:
Oh! John, John, John, the grey goose is gone,
And the fox is off to his den O!
    Den O! Den O!
Oh! John, John, John, the grey goose is gone,
And the fox is off to his den O!

John ran up to the top of the hill,
And blew his whistle loud and shrill;
Said the fox, That is very pretty music; still –
I'd rather be in my den O!
    Den O! Den O!
Said the fox, That is very pretty music; still –
I'd rather be in my den O!

The fox went back to his hungry den,
And his dear little foxes, eight, nine, ten;
Quoth they, Good Daddy, you must go there again,
If you bring such cheer from the farm O!
    Farm O! Farm O!
Quoth they, Good Daddy, you must go there again,
If you bring such cheer from the farm O!

The fox and his wife, without any strife,
Said they never ate a better goose in all their life:
They did very well without fork or knife,
And the little ones picked the bones O!
    Bones O! Bones O!
They did very well without fork or knife,
And the little ones picked the bones O!

THE ANIMAL FAIR

I went to the animal fair,
The birds and beasts were there.
The big baboon, by the light of the moon,
Was combing his auburn hair.
The monkey, he got drunk,
And sat on the elephant's trunk.
The elephant sneezed and fell on his knees,
And what became of the monk, the monk?

THERE WAS A LITTLE BOY

There was a little boy went into a barn,
  And lay down on some hay;
An owl came out and flew about,
  And the little boy ran away.

THERE WAS AN OLD MAN ON WHOSE NOSE

There was an Old Man on whose nose,
Most birds of the air could repose;
But they all flew away
At the closing of day,
  Which relieved that Old Man and his nose.

Edward Lear

THERE WAS A PIG

There was a Pig, that sat alone,
   Beside a ruined pump.
By day and night he made his moan:
It would have stirred a heart of stone
   To see him wring his hoofs and groan,
Because he could not jump.

Lewis Carroll

THERE WAS A LADY

There was a lady loved a swine:
   "Honey," quoth she,
"Pig-hog, wilt thou be mine?"
   "Grunt," quoth he.

"I'll build thee a silver sty,
   "Honey," quoth she,
"And in it thou shalt lie."
   "Grunt," quoth he.

"Pinned with a silver pin,
   "Honey," quoth she,
"That you may go out and in."
   "Grunt," quoth he.

"Wilt thou now have me,
   "Honey?" quoth she.
"Grunt, grunt, grunt," quoth he,
   And went his way.

HODDLEY, PODDLEY

Hoddley, poddley, puddle and fogs,
Cats are to marry the poodle dogs;
Cats in blue jackets and dogs in red hats,
What will become of the mice and the rats?

BIRDS OF A FEATHER

Birds of a feather flock together,
    And so will pigs and swine;
Rats and mice will have their choice,
    And so will I have mine.

LEG OVER LEG

Leg over leg.
    As the dog went to Dover,
When he came to a stile,
    Jump – he went over.

TWO LITTLE DOGS

Two little dogs
    Sat by the fire
Over a fender of coal dust;
    Said one little dog
    To the other little dog,
If you don't talk, why, I must.

THERE WAS A YOUNG MAN

There was a young man of Bengal
Who went to a fancy-dress ball,
He went, just for fun,
Dressed up as a bun,
And a dog ate him up in the hall.

JOHN AND A CHIMPANZEE

John and a chimpanzee
Sitting on a rail.
What is the difference?
John has no tail.

WHAT A WONDERFUL BIRD

What a wonderful bird the frog are!
When he stand he sit almost;
When he hop he fly almost.
He ain't got no sense hardly;
He ain't got no tail hardly either.
When he sit, he sit on what he ain't got almost.

THERE WAS AN OLD WOMAN

There was an old woman sat spinning,
And that's the first beginning;
   She had a calf,
   And that's half,
She took it by the tail,
And threw it over the wall,
And that's all.

THERE WAS A YOUNG MAIDEN

There was a young maiden called Maggie
Whose dog was hairy and shaggy;
The front end of him
Was vicious and grim
But the tail end was friendly and waggy.

THERE WAS A LITTLE DOG

There was a little dog and he had a tail
And he used to wag, wag, wag it!
But when he was sad, because he'd been bad,
On the ground he would drag, drag, drag it!

I'VE GOT A DOG

I've got a dog as thin as a rail,
He's got fleas all over his tail;
Every time his tail goes flop,
The fleas on the bottom all hop to the top.

DING, DONG, DARROW

Ding, dong, darrow,
The cat and the sparrow;
The little dog has burnt his tail,
And he shall be whipped tomorrow.

UP IN THE NORTH

Up in the North, a long way off,
The donkey's got the whooping cough;
He whooped so hard with the whooping cough,
He whooped his head and tail right off.

WIGGLE WAGGLE, WIGGLE WAGGLE

There was a little dog sitting by the fireside;
Out popped a little coal,
And in the little doggie's tail
It burnt a little hole.
Away ran the little dog, to seek a little pool
To cool his little tail,
And for want of a better place,
He popped it in the pail,
He popped it in the pail,
And wiggle waggle, wiggle waggle,
    wiggle waggle, wiggle waggle,
Went the doggie's tail.

PUSSY SITS BESIDE THE FIRE

Pussy sits beside the fire,
    So pretty and so fair.
In walks the little dog,
    Ah, pussy, are you there?
How do you do, Mistress Pussy?
    Mistress Pussy, how do you do?
I thank you kindly, little dog,
    I'm very well just now.

I HAD A LITTLE HEN

I had a little hen,
    The prettiest ever seen;
She washed up the dishes,
    And kept the house clean.
She went to the mill
    To fetch me some flour,
And always got home
    In less than an hour.
She baked me my bread,
    She brewed me my ale,
She sat by the fire
    And told a fine tale.

DAME TROT AND HER CAT

Dame Trot and her cat
Sat down for to chat;
The Dame sat on this side,
And Puss sat on that.

"Puss," says the Dame,
"Can you catch a rat,
Or a mouse in the dark?"
"Purr," says the cat.

THE SOW CAME IN

The sow came in with the saddle,
The little pig rocked the cradle,
  The dish jumped up on the table,
  To see the pot swallow the ladle.
The spit that stood behind the door
Threw the pudding-stick on the floor.
  Odd's-bobs! says the gridiron,
    Can't you agree?
  I'm the head constable,
    Bring them to me.

OUR YAK

We are very depressed with our yak,
Which has now become terribly slak.
It cleaned kitchens and stairs
Better than many au pairs,
But now we're going to send our yak bak.

I HAVE BEEN TO MARKET

I have been to market, my lady, my lady;
Then you've not been to the fair,
  says pussy, says pussy;
I bought me a rabbit, my lady, my lady;
Then you did not buy a hare,
  says pussy, says pussy;
I roasted it, my lady, my lady;
Then you did not boil it,
  says pussy, says pussy;
I eat it, my lady, my lady;
And I'll eat you,
  says pussy, says pussy.

I HAD A LITTLE DOG

I had a little dog and his name was Blue Bell,
I gave him some work, and he did it very well;
I sent him upstairs to pick up a pin,
He stepped in the coal-scuttle up to his chin;
I sent him to the garden to pick some sage,
He tumbled down and fell in a rage;
I sent him to the cellar to draw a pot of beer,
He came up again and said there was none there.

HEY DIDDLE DOUBT

Hey diddle doubt, my candle's out,
My little maid is not at home;
Saddle my hog and bridle my dog,
And fetch my little maid home.

RIDE AWAY

Ride away, ride away,
  Johnny shall ride,
He shall have a pussy cat
  Tied to one side.
He shall have a little dog
  Tied to the other
And Johnny shall ride
  To see his grandmother.

LITTLE JOHNNY MORGAN

Little Johnny Morgan,
  Gentleman of Wales,
Came riding on a nanny-goat,
  Selling of pigs' tails.

A FARMER WENT TROTTING

A farmer went trotting upon his grey mare,
    Bumpety, bumpety, bump!
With his daughter behind him so rosy and fair,
    Lumpety, lumpety, lump!

A raven cried, Croak! and they all tumbled down,
    Bumpety, bumpety, bump!
The mare broke her knees and the farmer his crown,
    Lumpety, lumpety, lump!

The mischievous raven flew laughing away,
    Bumpety, bumpety, bump!
And vowed he would serve them the same the next day,
    Lumpety, lumpety, lump!

AN OLD GREY HORSE

An old grey horse stood on the wall,
As daft as he was high.
He had no fear of falling down,
He thought he was a fly.

WHOOPS!

A horse and a flea and three blind mice
Sat on a curbstone shooting dice.
The horse he slipped and fell on the flea.
The flea said, "Whoops, there's a horse on me."

LITTLE FLY

Little fly upon the wall,
Ain't you got no clothes at all?
Ain't you got no shimmy shirt?
Ain't you got no petti-skirt?
Brrrrrr! Ain't you cold?

A BUG AND A FLEA

A bug and a flea
Went to sea
On a reel of cotton.
The bug was drowned
The flea was found
Stuck to a mermaid's bottom.

ALGY MET A BEAR

Algy met a bear,
A bear met Algy.
The bear was bulgy,
The bulge was Algy.

A FLY AND A FLEA

A fly and a flea in a flue
Were imprisoned, so what could they do?
   Said the fly, "Let us flee!"
   "Let us fly!" said the flea,
And they flew through a flaw in the flue.

'ARRY'S 'AWK

'Arry 'ad an 'awk in an 'atbag
   An' the 'awk made an 'orrible row.
'Arry 'it the 'awk wiv an 'eavy 'ard 'ammer.
   'Arry ain't got an 'awk now.

FUZZY WUZZY

Fuzzy Wuzzy was a bear;
Fuzzy Wuzzy had no hair.
So Fuzzy Wuzzy wasn't fuzzy. Was he?

THREE GREY GEESE

Three grey geese in a green field grazing
Grey were the geese and green was the grazing.

MY DAME

My dame hath a lame tame crane,
My dame hath a crane that is lame.
Pray, gentle Jane, let my dame's tame crane
Feed and come home again.

A.B.C.D. GOL'FISH?

A.B.C.D. Gol'fish?
M.N.O. Gol'fish
S.D.R. Gol'fish
R.D.R. Gol'fish!

THERE WAS A MAN

There was a man,
  And his name was Dob,
And he had a wife,
  And her name was Mob.
And he had a dog,
  And he called it Bob,
And she had a cat,
  Called Chitterabob.
    Bob, says Dob;
      Chitterabob, says Mob.
Bob was Dob's dog,
  Chitterabob Mob's cat.

THE QUANGLE WANGLE'S HAT

On the top of the Crumpetty Tree
   The Quangle Wangle sat,
But his face you could not see,
   On account of his Beaver Hat.
For his Hat was a hundred and two feet wide,
   With ribbons and bibbons on every side
And bells, and buttons, and loops, and lace,
   So that nobody ever could see the face
     Of the Quangle Wangle Quee.

The Quangle Wangle said
   To himself on the Crumpetty Tree, –
"Jam; and jelly; and bread;
   "Are the best food for me!
"But the longer I live on this Crumpetty Tree,
"The plainer than ever it seems to me
"That very few people come this way
"And that life on the whole is far from gay!"
   Said the Quangle Wangle Quee.

But there came to the Crumpetty Tree,
   Mr and Mrs Canary;
And they said – "Did you ever see
   "Any spot so charmingly airy?
"May we build a nest on your lovely Hat?
"Mr Quangle Wangle, grant us that!
"O please let us come and build a nest
"Of whatever material suits you best,
   "Mr Quangle Wangle Quee!"

And besides, to the Crumpetty Tree
   Came the Stork, the Duck, and the Owl;
The Snail, and the Bumble-Bee,
   The Frog, and the Fimble Fowl;
   (The Fimble Fowl, with a Corkscrew leg);
And all of them said, – "We humbly beg,
   "We may build our homes on your lovely Hat, –
   "Mr Quangle Wangle, grant us that!
   "Mr Quangle Wangle Quee!"

And the Golden Grouse came there,
   And the Pobble who has no toes, –
And the small Olympian bear, –
   And the Dong with a luminous nose.
And the Blue Baboon, who played the flute, –
And the Orient Calf from the Land of Tute, –
And the Attery Squash, and the Bisky Bat, –
All came and built on the lovely Hat
   Of the Quangle Wangle Quee.

And the Quangle Wangle said
   To himself on the Crumpetty Tree –
"When all these creatures move
   "What a wonderful noise there'll be!"
And at night by the light of the Mulberry moon
They danced to the Flute of the Blue Baboon,
On the broad green leaves of the Crumpetty Tree,
And all were as happy as happy could be,
   With the Quangle Wangle Quee.

Edward Lear

TWINKLE, TWINKLE, LITTLE BAT!

Twinkle, twinkle, little bat!
How I wonder what you're at!
Up above the world you fly,
Like a tea-tray in the sky.
  Twinkle, twinkle –

Lewis Carroll

ARYMOUSE, ARYMOUSE

Arymouse, arymouse, fly over my head,
And you shall ha' a crust o' bread;
And when I brew and when I bake,
You shall ha' a piece of my wedding cake.

BAT, BAT

Bat, bat,
    Come under my hat,
  And I'll give you a slice of bacon;
And when I bake,
I'll give you a cake,
  If I am not mistaken.

I HAD A CAT

I had a cat and the cat pleased me,
I fed my cat by yonder tree;
   Cat goes fiddle-i-fee.

I had a hen and the hen pleased me,
I fed my hen by yonder tree;
   Hen goes chimmy-chuck, chimmy-chuck,
   Cat goes fiddle-i-fee.

I had a duck and the duck pleased me,
I fed my duck by yonder tree;
   Duck goes quack, quack,
   Hen goes chimmy-chuck, chimmy-chuck,
   Cat goes fiddle-i-fee.

I had a goose and the goose pleased me,
I fed my goose by yonder tree;
   Goose goes swishy, swashy,
   Duck goes quack, quack,
   Hen goes chimmy-chuck, chimmy-chuck,
   Cat goes fiddle-i-fee.

I had a sheep and the sheep pleased me,
I fed my sheep by yonder tree;
   Sheep goes baa, baa,
   Goose goes swishy, swashy,
   Duck goes quack, quack,
   Hen goes chimmy-chuck, chimmy-chuck,
   Cat goes fiddle-i-fee.

I had a pig and the pig pleased me,
I fed my pig by yonder tree;
   Pig goes griffy, gruffy,
   Sheep goes baa, baa,
   Goose goes swishy, swashy,
   Duck goes quack, quack,
   Hen goes chimmy-chuck, chimmy-chuck,
   Cat goes fiddle-i-fee.

I had a cow and the cow pleased me,
I fed my cow by yonder tree;
    Cow goes moo, moo,
    Pig goes griffy, gruffy,
    Sheep goes baa, baa,
    Goose goes swishy, swashy,
    Duck goes quack, quack,
    Hen goes chimmy-chuck, chimmy-chuck,
    Cat goes fiddle-i-fee.

I had a horse and the horse pleased me,
I fed my horse by yonder tree;
    Horse goes neigh, neigh,
    Cow goes moo, moo,
    Pig goes griffy, gruffy,
    Sheep goes baa, baa,
    Goose goes swishy, swashy,
    Duck goes quack, quack,
    Hen goes chimmy-chuck, chimmy-chuck,
    Cat goes fiddle-i-fee.

I had a dog and the dog pleased me,
I fed my dog by yonder tree;
    Dog goes bow-wow, bow-wow,
    Horse goes neigh, neigh,
    Cow goes moo, moo,
    Pig goes griffy, gruffy,
    Sheep goes baa, baa,
    Goose goes swishy, swashy,
    Duck goes quack, quack,
    Hen goes chimmy-chuck, chimmy-chuck,
    Cat goes fiddle-i-fee.

COCK, COCK, COCK, COCK

Cock: Hen, hen, hen, hen,
I've been up and down,
To every shop in town,
And cannot find a shoe
To fit your foot,
If I'd crow my hea-art out.

Hen: Cock, cock, cock, cock,
I've laid an egg,
Am I to go ba-are foot?

THIS PIG GOT IN THE BARN

This pig got in the barn,

This ate all the corn,

This said he wasn't well,

This said he'd go and tell,

And this said – weke, weke, weke,
I can't get over the barn door sill.

HIGGLETY, PIGGLETY, POP!

Higglety, pigglety, pop!
The dog has eaten the mop;
   The pig's in a hurry,
   The cat's in a flurry,
Higglety, pigglety, pop!

Samuel Goodrich

OUR KITTEN

Our kitten, the one we call Louie,
Will never eat liver so chewy,
Nor the milk, nor the fish
That we put in his dish,
He only will dine on chop suey.

ONCE THERE LIVED A LITTLE MAN

Once there lived a little man
Where a little river ran,
And he had a little farm and a little dairy O!
And he had a little plough,
And a little dappled cow,
Which he often called his pretty little fairy O!

And his dog he called Fidele,
For he loved his master well,
And he had a little pony for his pleasure O!
In a sty, not very big,
He'd a frisky little pig
Which he often called his little piggy treasure O!

I HAD A LITTLE COW

I had a little cow: to save her,
I turned her into the meadow to graze her;

The bell-ropes they were made of hay,
And the little cow ate them all away;

There came a heavy storm of rain,
And drove the little cow home again.

The sexton came to toll the bell,
And pushed the little cow into the well!

The church doors they stood open,
And there the little cow was cropen;

THERE WAS AN OLD MAN WHO SAID

There was an Old Man who said, "How
Shall I flee from that horrible cow?
I will sit on this stile
And continue to smile,
　Which may soften the heart of that cow."

Edward Lear

THE PURPLE COW

I never saw a purple cow,
I never hope to see one;
But I can tell you, any how,
I'd rather see than be one.

THERE WAS A RAT

There was a rat, for want of stairs,
Went down a rope to say his prayers.

JERRY HALL

Jerry Hall,
He is so small,
A rat could eat him,
Hat and all.

HE WAS A RAT, AND SHE WAS A RAT

He was a rat, and she was a rat,
And down in one hole they did dwell,
And both were as black as a witch's cat,
And they loved each other well.

He had a tail, and she had a tail,
Both long and curling and fine;
And each said, "Yours is the finest tail
In the world, excepting mine."

He smelt the cheese, and she smelt the cheese,
And they both pronounced it good;
And both remarked it would greatly add
To the charms of their daily food.

So he ventured out, and she ventured out,
And I saw them go with pain;
But what befell them I never can tell,
For they never came back again.

THREE YOUNG RATS

Three young rats with black felt hats,
Three young ducks with white straw flats,
Three young dogs with curling tails,
Three young cats with demi-veils,
Went out to walk with two young pigs
In satin vests and sorrel wigs;
But suddenly it chanced to rain,
And so they all went home again.

THE COMMON CORMORANT

The common cormorant or shag
Lays eggs inside a paper bag
The reason you will see no doubt –
It is to keep the lightning out.
But what these unobservant birds
Have never noticed is that herds
Of wandering bears may come with buns
And steal the bags to hold the crumbs.

A WISE OLD OWL

A wise old owl sat in an oak,
The more he heard the less he spoke;
The less he spoke the more he heard.
Why aren't we all like that wise old bird?

BE LENIENT WITH LOBSTERS

Be lenient with lobsters, and even kind to crabs,
And be not disrespectful to cuttlefish or dabs;
Chase not the Cochin-China, chaff not the ox obese,
And babble not of feather-beds in company with geese.
Be tender with the tadpole, and let the limpet thrive,
Be merciful to mussels, don't skin your eels alive;
When talking to a turtle don't mention calipee –
Be always kind to animals wherever you may be.

THE LION

The lion, the lion, he dwells in the waste,
He has a big head and a very small waist;
But his shoulders are stark, and his jaws they are grim,
And a good little child will not play with him.

Hilaire Belloc

SOME RABBITS

Some rabbits came over from Arden
And gobbled up most of my garden.
They feasted for hours
On stalks and on flowers
And never once said, "Beg your pardon."

THE FROG

Be kind and tender to the Frog,
    And do not call him names,
As "Slimy skin", or "Polly-wog",
    Or likewise "Ugly James",
Or "Gape-a-grin", or "Toad-gone-wrong",
    Or "Billy Bandy-knees":
The Frog is justly sensitive
    To epithets like these.
No animal will more repay
    A treatment kind and fair;
At least so lonely people say
Who keep a frog (and, by the way,
    They are extremely rare).

Hilaire Belloc

IF YOU SHOULD MEET A CROCODILE

If you should meet a crocodile,
Don't take a stick and poke him;
Ignore the welcome in his smile,
Be careful not to stroke him.
For as he sleeps upon the Nile,
He thinner gets and thinner;
And whene'er you meet a crocodile
He's ready for his dinner.

THE MONKEY AND THE DONKEY

Said the monkey to the donkey,
"What'll you have to drink?"
Said the donkey to the monkey,
"I'd like a swig of ink."

OLD-JUMPETY-BUMPETY-HOP-AND-GO-ONE

Old-Jumpety-Bumpety-Hop-and-Go-One
Was lying on his side in the sun.
This old kangaroo, he was whisking the flies
(With his glossy tail) from his ears and his eyes.
Jumpety-Bumpety-Hop-and-Go-One
Was lying asleep on his side in the sun,
Jumpety-Bumpety-Hop!

THE CROCODILE

How doth the little crocodile
   Improve his shining tail,
And pour the waters of the Nile
   On every golden scale!

How cheerfully he seems to grin!
   How neatly spread his claws,
And welcomes little fishes in
   With gently smiling jaws!

Lewis Carroll

THE ROBIN AND THE WREN

The robin and the wren,
They fought upon the porridge pan;
But ere the robin got a spoon,
The wren had eat the porridge down.

LITTLE CLOTILDA

Little Clotilda,
    Well and hearty,
Thought she'd like
    To give a party.
But as her friends
    Were shy and wary,
Nobody came
    But her own canary.

THERE WERE TWO BIRDS

There were two birds sat on a stone,
    Fa, la, la, la, lal, de;
One flew away, and then there was one,
    Fa, la, la, la, lal, de;
The other flew after, and then there was none,
    Fa, la, la, la, lal, de;
And so the poor stone was left all alone,
    Fa, la, la, la, lal, de.

THERE WAS AN OLD MAN OF DUMBREE

There was an Old Man of Dumbree,
Who taught little Owls to drink Tea;
For he said, "To eat mice
Is not proper or nice,"
    That amiable Man of Dumbree.

Edward Lear

THERE WAS AN OLD MAN WITH A BEARD

There was an Old Man with a beard
Who said, "It is just as I feared! –
    Four Larks and a Wren,
    Two Owls and a Hen,
Have all built their nests in my beard!"

Edward Lear

BUT I DUNNO

I sometimes think I'd rather crow
And be a rooster than to roost
And be a crow. But I dunno.

A rooster he can roost also,
Which don't seem fair when crows can't crow
Which may help some. But I dunno.

Crows should be glad of one thing though;
Nobody thinks of eating crow,
While roosters they are good enough
For anyone unless they're tough.

There's lots of tough old roosters though,
And anyway a crow can't crow,
So mebby roosters stand more show.
It looks that way. But I dunno.

Index of first lines

MORE WALKER PAPERBACKS
For You to Enjoy

BIRDS BEASTS AND FISHES
Compiled by Anne Carter / illustrated by Reg Cartwright

An entertaining anthology of over fifty poems on creatures of all
shapes and sizes, colours and character by some of the finest poets
from across the ages – from Aesop to Blake, Edward Lear to Ted Hughes.

"Wonderfully bold, colourful, naive and
witty pictures… A lovely book." *The School Librarian*

0-7445-3056-3   £4.99

A CUP OF STARSHINE
Retold by Jill Bennett / illustrated by Graham Percy

In this lively and varied anthology for young children you'll
find poems about washing, dressing, eating and playing; poems about the sun
and the moon, winter winds and springtime – poems as mouthwatering
and mysterious as a cup of starshine.

"A beautifully produced and illustrated anthology." *The Independent on Sunday*

0-7445-3040-7   £5.99

OUR VILLAGE
by John Yeoman / Quentin Blake

A delightful volume of illustrated verse about village life in days gone by.

"Some of Quentin Blake's best illustrations ever… Gloriously full of amusing detail…
Sparkling fun. A delightful double-act." *Books for Keeps*

0-7445-1371-5   £3.99